Code Craft

The Programmer's Mindset

Empower Your Mind, Code with Resilience and Precision

by

Oladeji Afolabi

The Programmer's Mindset

© 2023 by Oladeji Afolabi

TABLE OF CONTENTS

Code Craft: The Programmer's Mindset

Empower Your Mind, Code with Resilience and Precision

Introduction

Code Craft: The Programmer's Mindset is a book that takes readers on an extraordinary journey into the heart of technology. It explores the secrets of exceptional developers who navigate the intricate mazes of binary brilliance with ease, focusing on logical thinking, problem-solving prowess, and perpetual learning. The book also explores the delicate balance between creativity and precision, as programmers seamlessly weave their lines of code into masterpieces of functionality and elegance.

Coding is not a solitary endeavor; it's a symphony of collaboration, where programmers embrace the melodies created by their peers. The book uncovers the secrets of effective teamwork, exploring the alchemy that occurs when minds intertwine, merging their brilliance into a collective powerhouse. It also discusses strategies to combat distractions and optimize productivity, ensuring a harmonious life as a programmer.

The book also unveils the resilient mindset that fuels the passion for programming and guarantees a harmonious work-life equilibrium. It banishes the notion of the tortured programmer, allowing for a tapestry of balance where work and play coexist in blissful harmony, allowing for a thriving life as both a human being and a programmer.

In Code Craft: The Programmer's Mindset, readers embark on an extraordinary voyage where logic dances with creativity, bonds are forged, and time bends to our will. Join us in this symphony of coding brilliance, where the magic of programming unfolds before your very eyes.

Chapter 1: The Foundation of Code Craft

The Power of Logical Thinking

When it comes to programming, logic is the foundation upon which everything is built. It is the key that unlocks the door to solving complex problems and creating elegant solutions. As a programmer, your ability to think logically and reason through the code can make the difference between success and failure.

Logical thinking is the ability to analyze and reason through information in a clear and systematic way. It allows you to break down complex problems into manageable pieces, identify patterns, and make informed decisions. In the world of programming, logical thinking is the driving force behind creating efficient algorithms, debugging code, and finding innovative solutions.

One of the fundamental types of logical reasoning is deductive reasoning. This is the process of using general principles or rules to reach specific conclusions. In programming, it involves applying known facts or rules to solve a particular problem. For example, if you know that all mammals have hair and a dog is a mammal, you can deduce that a dog has hair. Deductive reasoning is crucial in programming because it helps us understand how different parts of a program work together and how they produce specific outputs.

Another type of logical reasoning is inductive reasoning. Unlike deductive reasoning, which starts with general principles, inductive reasoning starts with specific observations or evidence and uses them to make generalizations or predictions. In programming, this type of reasoning is often used when analyzing data and finding patterns. For example, if you observe that all the numbers in a sequence are increasing by the same amount, you can use inductive reasoning to predict the next number in the sequence. Inductive reasoning is especially useful when dealing with large amounts of data or complex systems.

Developing strong logical thinking skills is crucial for any programmer. Fortunately, there are techniques that can help you enhance your logical thinking abilities and apply them to real-world coding challenges. One of these techniques is breaking down problems into smaller, more manageable pieces. By dividing a complex problem into smaller sub-problems, you can focus on solving each piece individually and then combine the solutions to create a comprehensive solution.

Another technique is using flowcharts or pseudo-code to visualize and plan your solutions. Flowcharts are graphical representations of the steps involved in solving a problem, while pseudo-code is a simplified version of code that describes the logic of a program without the need for specific syntax. Both of these tools can help you see the logical flow of your program and identify any potential issues or inefficiencies.

Additionally, practicing abstraction can sharpen your logical thinking skills. Abstraction is the process of simplifying complex problems by focusing on the essential elements and ignoring the irrelevant details. By abstracting away unnecessary details, you can better understand the core logic of a problem and design more efficient and maintainable code.

Furthermore, learning to think systematically can greatly enhance your logical thinking abilities. This involves approaching problems in a structured and methodical way, breaking them down into smaller steps and analyzing each step comprehensively. It also includes constantly evaluating and revisiting your solutions to ensure they align with the problem requirements and produce the desired outcomes.

Logical thinking in programming goes beyond simply following a set of rules or guidelines. It requires intuition and creativity to find innovative solutions to complex problems. As a programmer, you must constantly challenge yourself to think outside the box and explore different possibilities. This might involve experimenting with different approaches, considering alternative solutions, or even seeking inspiration from other domains.

To develop and maintain your logical thinking skills, continuous learning and practice are essential. Stay up-to-date with the latest programming concepts, languages, and techniques. Engage in coding challenges, participate in online communities, and collaborate with other programmers. Surround yourself with like-minded individuals who can inspire and challenge you to think critically and creatively.

In conclusion, logical thinking is the backbone of programming. It enables you to analyze problems, identify patterns, and create innovative solutions. By understanding the different types of logical reasoning, such as deductive and inductive reasoning, and incorporating techniques to enhance your logical thinking skills, you can excel in the world of programming. Remember to think systematically, practice abstraction, and continuously challenge yourself to think creatively. With a strong logical thinking mindset, you can tackle any coding challenge with confidence and create elegant and efficient solutions.

Mastering the Art of Problem-Solving

As a programmer, the ability to solve problems efficiently and effectively is a crucial skill that sets you apart from the rest. In this section, we will delve deep into the world of problem-solving and explore various strategies and techniques that will help you approach complex coding problems with confidence and creativity.

The Foundation of Problem-Solving

Before we dive into the different problem-solving strategies, it is important to understand the foundation upon which effective problem-solving is built. As a seasoned data analyst and software developer, I have encountered my fair share of challenging coding problems. Through my experience, I have come to realize that problem-solving is not just about finding a solution; it is about understanding the problem itself and breaking it down into manageable pieces.

In order to master the art of problem-solving, it is essential to develop a systematic approach. This involves analyzing the problem, identifying the key components, and formulating a plan of attack. By following this structured process, you can avoid getting overwhelmed by the complexity of the problem and tackle it one step at a time.

Divide and Conquer

One of the most effective problem-solving strategies in the world of programming is divide and conquer. This strategy involves breaking down a complex problem into smaller, more manageable sub-problems. By tackling each sub-problem individually, you can gradually build up towards solving the larger problem.

Divide and conquer allows you to focus on specific aspects of the problem at hand, making it easier to understand and solve. This technique is particularly useful when dealing with large datasets or complex algorithms. By dividing the problem into smaller parts, you can identify patterns, relationships, and potential solutions that may not have been apparent before.

Pattern Recognition

Pattern recognition is another powerful problem-solving technique that can greatly enhance your coding skills. When faced with a problem, your ability to recognize patterns can help you identify similarities and repetitions that can be leveraged to find a solution.

Patterns can exist in various forms, such as data structures, algorithms, or even coding conventions. By recognizing these patterns, you can apply existing solutions to new problems, saving time and effort in the process. Additionally, pattern recognition allows you to spot errors or inefficiencies in your code, enabling you to optimize and improve your solutions.

Algorithmic Thinking

At the core of problem-solving in programming lies algorithmic thinking. Algorithms are step-by-step logical procedures that outline the sequence of operations required to solve a problem. Developing strong algorithmic thinking skills is essential for efficiently solving complex coding problems.

Algorithmic thinking involves breaking down a problem into its fundamental components and designing a logical sequence of steps to solve it. This requires a deep understanding of the problem domain, the ability to think critically, and a creative mindset to come up with innovative solutions.

Approaching Complex Problems

Complex coding problems can often be intimidating, but with the right mindset and approach, they can be conquered. When faced with a complex problem, it is important to remain calm and approach it methodically.

First, take the time to fully understand the problem and its requirements. Break it down into smaller sub-problems and identify any patterns or similarities that can be leveraged to find a solution. Then, apply the appropriate problem-solving strategies, such as divide and conquer or pattern recognition, to tackle each sub-problem individually.

By approaching complex problems with confidence, creativity, and a growth mindset, you will develop the skills and mindset necessary to excel in the world of programming.

Conclusion

Problem-solving is not just a technical skill; it is a mindset that encompasses creativity, critical thinking, and perseverance. By mastering the art of problem-solving, you can overcome even the most challenging coding problems with confidence and efficiency.

Embracing Continuous Learning

As someone deeply entrenched in the tech industry for over 18 years, I have witnessed firsthand the tremendous value that continuous learning brings to one's professional development. The rapid rate at which technology is advancing requires individuals to adapt and learn new skills consistently. Without an unwavering commitment to learning, it becomes increasingly difficult to keep up with the latest trends and remain competitive in the job market.

Strategies for staying updated with the latest programming languages and best practices are plentiful in the digital age. Online resources have revolutionized the way we acquire knowledge, making it easier than ever to access tutorials, documentation, and online courses. Websites such as StackOverflow, GitHub, and YouTube offer a wealth of information, enabling us to learn new concepts and solve coding problems with a few clicks, even with AI's like chatGPT.

Mentorship is another powerful tool for continuous learning. Finding a mentor who is experienced in your field can provide valuable guidance, help avoid common pitfalls, and accelerate your learning curve. A mentor can offer advice on best practices, challenge your thinking, and provide constructive feedback on your work. Building a relationship with a mentor allows you to tap into their wealth of experience and gain insights that might otherwise take years to acquire.

Technology is a field that demands constant adaptation. As programmers, we must not only embrace continuous learning, but also ensure that we are learning the right things. While it can be tempting to jump on every new bandwagon, it is important to identify and focus on areas that align with our goals and interests.

As I reflect on my own journey, I realize that embracing continuous learning has been the driving force behind my success in the tech industry. It has allowed me to remain agile and adaptable in the face of constant change, and to consistently deliver exceptional results.

Chapter 2: The Creative Coder

The Beauty of Clean Code

As I dive into the world of clean code, I am reminded of the famous quote by Robert C. Martin, a renowned software engineer: "Clean code always looks like it was written by someone who cares." These words perfectly encapsulate the essence of clean code - the attention to detail, the meticulousness, and the care that goes into crafting software that is not only functional but also maintainable and readable.

In this chapter, we will explore the importance of clean code and how it can revolutionize the way we approach software development. We will delve into coding practices that can significantly enhance the quality of our code, such as meaningful variable names, modularization, and code commenting. Additionally, we will uncover techniques to refactor existing code, improving its clarity and efficiency.

Join me on this journey as we discover the beauty of clean code and its power to transform our programming mindset.

The Power of Meaningful Variable Names:

One of the most fundamental aspects of clean code is the use of meaningful variable names. We've all seen the countless examples of code filled with cryptic and obscure variable names that make it nearly impossible to understand the purpose and functionality of the code. However, by choosing descriptive and self-explanatory variable names, we can greatly improve the readability and maintainability of our code.

Consider the following example:

int p; // Poor choice of variable name

int numberOfProducts; // Meaningful variable name

By using variable names that convey the purpose and intent of the data they represent, we can instantly grasp the meaning of the code. This not only benefits us as the developers but also future team members who may need to understand and modify our code.

The Art of Modularization:

Modularization is an essential principle of clean code. Breaking down complex code into smaller, manageable modules not only improves readability but also makes it easier to test, maintain, and reuse code. Each module should have a clearly defined responsibility, making it easier to understand and modify independently.

When we modularize our code, we promote the concept of "single responsibility," where each module focuses on a specific functionality or task. By doing this, we reduce the complexity of the codebase and make it easier to identify and isolate bugs or issues.

Imagine having a large codebase with numerous functions and classes all mashed together. It would be like searching for a needle in a haystack when trying to debug or enhance that code. However, by breaking it down into modular components, we create a codebase that is more manageable, maintainable, and comprehensible.

The Importance of Code Commenting:

Code commenting is often undervalued and overlooked, but it plays a crucial role in clean code development. By providing clear and concise comments, we can improve the understandability of our code and assist future developers in comprehending its inner workings.

When we comment our code, we are essentially leaving behind a roadmap for others to follow. We can explain complex algorithms, describe the purpose of specific sections of code, and highlight any potential pitfalls.

However, it is essential to strike a delicate balance when commenting code. Too many comments can clutter the code and make it difficult to read, while too few comments may leave developers scratching their heads. Therefore, we must adopt a mindful approach to code commenting, providing enough information to guide others while not overwhelming the codebase.

The Power of Refactoring:

Refactoring is the process of improving the structure, readability, and efficiency of existing code without changing its functionality. It is an essential discipline in the world of clean code as it allows us to continuously enhance our codebase over time.

By refactoring our code, we eliminate unnecessary duplication, enhance variable names and function clarity, remove dead code, and improve performance. It is a powerful practice that can transform mediocre code into elegant and efficient code.

When refactoring, we need to ensure that we have strong test coverage to avoid introducing new bugs or regressions. We must also adopt an incremental approach, refactoring small portions of code at a time, to minimize the impact on the overall system.

Innovation Through Code

In today's fast-paced digital age, the role of code in driving innovation cannot be underestimated. Code has become the language of innovation, enabling us to transform ideas into reality and reshape the world around us.

To truly innovate through code, it requires a mindset that embraces curiosity, experimentation, and a willingness to challenge established norms. It is about thinking beyond the confines of traditional solutions and exploring new ways to solve problems. This mindset is essential for staying ahead in a rapidly evolving technological landscape.

Learning how to think outside the box is a crucial aspect of the programmer's mindset. It involves breaking free from conventional patterns of thinking and exploring unconventional ideas. It is about questioning assumptions and looking for alternative approaches. By pushing the boundaries of what is considered possible, we can discover innovative solutions that have the potential to revolutionize industries.

One example of thinking outside the box is the development of self-driving cars. Traditional transportation systems relied on human drivers and required significant infrastructure. However, by leveraging the power of code and artificial intelligence, companies like Tesla and Waymo have developed autonomous vehicle technology that has the potential to transform the way we travel.

These self-driving cars use a combination of sensors, data analysis, and machine learning algorithms to navigate the roads safely and efficiently. Through continuous experimentation and refinement, they have overcome challenges such as real-time decision-making, object recognition, and adapting to unpredictable road conditions. The innovation lies in the ability to merge code with cutting-edge technology, creating a system that can learn, adapt, and ultimately revolutionize the transportation industry.

Another area where code has fueled innovation is in the field of healthcare. Traditional methods of diagnosing and treating diseases often relied on manual processes and subjective assessments. However, with the advent of code-driven technologies, we have seen a shift towards more precise and efficient healthcare solutions.

One such example is the use of deep learning algorithms to analyze medical images and detect diseases such as cancer. Code-driven software can analyze vast amounts of data and identify patterns that may not be discernible to the human eye. This innovation has the potential to significantly improve early detection rates and save countless lives.

In addition to thinking outside the box, innovation through code also involves experimenting with new technologies. It requires a mindset that embraces change and is willing to explore uncharted territories. By staying up to date with the latest advancements in technology, programmers can position themselves at the forefront of innovation.

One area where constant experimentation and exploration of new technologies is crucial is in web development. The Internet is an ever-evolving landscape, and staying ahead requires adapting to emerging trends and technologies. As a programmer, I have always been fascinated by the potential of web applications and the opportunities they present for innovation.

One example of experimenting with new technologies in web development is the rise of Progressive Web Apps (PWAs). PWAs combine the best features of both web and mobile applications, providing users with a seamless and engaging experience. By utilizing modern web technologies such as service workers, push notifications, and offline caching, PWAs have the potential to transform the way we interact with the Internet.

The power of code to drive innovation can also be seen in the gaming industry. Video games have come a long way since the early days of simple 8-bit graphics. Today, game developers are using sophisticated code-driven technologies to create immersive and realistic gaming experiences.

One such innovation is the use of virtual reality (VR) and augmented reality (AR) in gaming. By leveraging code to create virtual worlds and interactive experiences, game developers have transformed the gaming industry. Players can now step into a virtual world and experience games in a way that was once unimaginable.

The impact of code-driven innovation is not limited to specific industries. It has the potential to revolutionize various sectors, from finance to agriculture to manufacturing. By embracing the programmer's mindset and pushing the boundaries of what is possible, we can unlock new opportunities and create a better future.

In conclusion, innovation through code is about unleashing your creativity, thinking outside the box, and exploring the possibilities of new technologies. It requires a mindset that embraces curiosity, experimentation, and a willingness to challenge established norms.

The Simplicity Paradigm

When it comes to programming, one of the most important principles to adhere to is the concept of simplicity. As programmers, we often find ourselves navigating through complex and intricate problems, and it is easy to fall into the trap of making our code equally convoluted. However, understanding and embracing the power of simplicity can transform the way we approach coding and design, leading to more elegant and efficient solutions.

In the world of programming, simplicity can be defined as the art of eliminating unnecessary complexity, reducing code duplication, and creating elegant solutions that are easy to understand and maintain. It is about finding the most straightforward and efficient way to solve a problem, rather than getting lost in a maze of convoluted logic.

One of the key benefits of simplicity is readability. When code is simple and easy to understand, it becomes much easier for other programmers to decipher its purpose and functionality. In a collaborative environment, this can greatly enhance team productivity and communication. Furthermore, readable code is not only beneficial for fellow programmers but also for your future self. As time goes by, you may need to revisit and modify your code, and simplicity ensures that you can quickly understand and make changes to it without wasting unnecessary time and effort.

Maintainability is another advantage of simplicity. When code is complex and convoluted, making changes and fixing bugs can become a time-consuming and error-prone task. On the other hand, when code is simple and easy to follow, it becomes much easier to identify and fix issues. By embracing simplicity, you can greatly reduce the chances of introducing new bugs during the maintenance phase and ensure that your code remains robust and reliable.

Another aspect to consider is the overall user experience. Users interact with software and applications on a daily basis, and simplicity plays a crucial role in making their experience smooth and enjoyable. A simple and intuitive user interface is much more likely to attract and retain users compared to a complex and confusing one. By implementing a simplicity paradigm in your design, you create interfaces that are easy to navigate, reducing the learning curve for users and increasing their satisfaction.

Chapter 3: The Collaborative Coder

Effective Communication in Teams

Effective communication is a critical aspect of any team setting, as it ensures that all team members understand the message and can work together effectively. Clear and concise language is essential, as miscommunication can lead to confusion, errors, and delays in project completion. Active listening, which involves being fully present and engaged in conversations, is another fundamental principle of effective communication. It allows for gathering information, understanding others' perspectives, concerns, and needs, and helps prevent misunderstandings and conflicts.

One technique to enhance active listening is paraphrasing, which involves summarizing the speaker's words and reflecting it back to them. This technique not only shows understanding but also allows the speaker to clarify any misconceptions or provide additional information.

Constructive feedback is another crucial aspect of effective communication in teams, as it improves performance, encourages personal and professional growth, and fosters a culture of continuous improvement. In a team setting, giving feedback requires tact, empathy, and a focus on solutions rather than criticism. Specific and objective feedback is essential, providing examples and explanations of what could be improved.

Timely feedback is crucial, as waiting too long can lead to resentment and misunderstandings, hindering the team's progress. Addressing concerns promptly prevents small issues from escalating into major problems and ensures everyone is aligned and working towards a common goal.

Conflicts are inevitable in a team, but how they are handled can significantly impact the team's effectiveness and cohesion. Effective communication plays a crucial role in conflict resolution, allowing team members to express their thoughts and feelings openly and honestly.

When conflicts arise, it is essential to remain calm and composed, as emotions can easily escalate tensions and hinder meaningful resolution. Active listening and constructive feedback can help create an environment where conflicts can be resolved amicably, acknowledging each person's feelings and concerns, seeking common ground, and working towards a solution that satisfies everyone involved.

Finally, fostering a positive and collaborative team environment requires promoting open and transparent communication, encouraging team members to share their thoughts, ideas, and concerns freely without fear of judgment or reprisal.

It's important to be open to criticism and aggressively seek out other people's opinions while creating a safe environment for dialogue. This not only exemplifies humility, but it also improves teamwork and trust. Team members are more likely to provide their best work and actively participate in the team's goals when they feel heard and valued.

In conclusion, good teamwork is built on efficient communication. You can improve your communication abilities and develop into a more influential and effective team member by adhering to the key principles described in this chapter, such as communicating clearly, actively listening, giving constructive criticism, resolving conflicts, and creating a positive team environment. As a result, there will be an increase in productivity, creativity, and collaboration, which will boost your professional success and sense of contentment.

Harnessing the Power of Version Control

In today's fast-paced and constantly evolving world of software development, collaboration is key. The ability to work seamlessly with a team, manage code changes, and track progress is crucial to the success of any project. This is where version control systems come into play. These powerful tools empower programmers to effectively collaborate on code, manage conflicts, and track changes in a team environment.

At the heart of version control systems lies the concept of preserving different versions of the codebase. With the advent of distributed version control systems like Git, managing code changes has become more efficient and convenient than ever before. Git, in particular, has grown in popularity due to its effectiveness in handling both small and large-scale projects.

Git, developed by Linus Torvalds in 2005, revolutionized the way developers manage their code. Its distributed nature allows for multiple developers to work on the same codebase simultaneously without fear of conflicts or losing previous versions. Creating a local repository on each developer's machine, enabling him or her to make changes independently and merge them seamlessly with the central repository when ready, does this.

One of the most significant advantages of using Git is its ability to handle conflicts gracefully. Conflicts often arise when multiple developers make changes to the same file or line of code simultaneously. Git provides a mechanism to detect these conflicts and prompts developers to resolve them before merging their changes. This ensures that conflicts are resolved, and the final merged version of the code remains clean and error-free.

To effectively leverage the power of Git, developers need to familiarize themselves with its core concepts and commands. This includes understanding branches, commits, merging, and rebasing. Branches allow developers to work on separate features or bug fixes without affecting the main codebase. Commits serve as snapshots of code changes, providing a clear track of progress and a way to revert to previous versions if needed. Merging combines different branches together, while rebasing allows for a cleaner integration of changes from one branch to another.

Beyond Git, there are other popular version control tools, such as SVN (Subversion) and Mercurial. Each has its own strengths and weaknesses, making it essential for developers to choose the right tool based on their project requirements. However, Git's dominance in the industry and its vast community support make it an ideal choice for most collaborative coding projects.

GitHub is a platform that hosts Git repositories and offers various collaboration features, such as pull requests, issue tracking, code reviews, and project management tools. It streamlines the development process, making it easier for teams to collaborate, review code, and catch bugs early on. Code reviews are crucial in maintaining code quality and catching potential issues before they make their way into the final product. They involve team members reviewing each other's code, providing feedback, and suggesting improvements.

To excel in collaborative coding projects, it is essential to establish a consistent and efficient workflow, including defining coding standards, setting up continuous integration tools, and incorporating automated testing. This standardizes coding practices and automates repetitive tasks, saving time, reducing errors, and improving overall code quality.

One powerful technique to enhance collaboration using version control is the use of feature branches. These branches allow developers to work on new features or bug fixes independently without interfering with the main codebase. Effective communication within the team is crucial when using feature branches, with regular updates and status reports keeping everyone in the loop and preventing conflicts arising from simultaneous modifications in the same area of the codebase.

However, collaboration in coding projects is not without challenges. Managing conflicts, resolving differences in coding styles, and coordinating efforts across various time zones are just a few examples. Effective communication, mutual respect, and a shared vision are fundamental in overcoming these challenges and ensuring a productive and harmonious teamwork environment.

Collaborative coding projects thrive on version control systems, providing a foundation for teams to work together harmoniously, manage code changes efficiently, and produce exceptional results. By harnessing the power of version control tools like Git and leveraging platforms like GitHub, programmers can elevate their collaborative coding experience to new heights.

Remote Collaboration

Remote collaboration is a growing field that offers both opportunities and challenges. It allows teams to work with diverse individuals from around the world, but it also presents communication barriers and challenges in maintaining a cohesive team culture. To overcome these obstacles, it is crucial to use appropriate tools and techniques for effective remote communication, task management, and collaboration.

Effective communication is essential for successful remote collaboration, and tools like chat platforms, video conferencing, and project management software can help ensure everyone is on the same page. Establishing clear communication channels and response time expectations from the start can foster trust and accountability among team members. Task management tools like Asana or Trello can help track progress and keep everyone aligned, allowing team members to assign tasks, set deadlines, and monitor progress in real-time. Regular check-ins and status updates can further enhance transparency and accountability within the team.

Fostering a cohesive team culture is also vital in remote collaboration. Despite physical distance, it is essential to create a sense of camaraderie and shared goals through virtual team-building activities, regular team meetings, and informal social interactions. Team-building activities, such as online games and quizzes, provide an opportunity for team members to connect on a personal level and build trust. Regular team meetings, both for project updates and general discussions, maintain a sense of cohesiveness and align everyone towards common goals. Informal social interactions, such as using platforms like Slack or Microsoft Teams, can also foster relationships and create a positive team culture.

To succeed in a distributed team environment, it's essential to overcome the challenges of physical distance. Miscommunication is a common issue, often due to cultural differences and language barriers. To overcome this, adapt communication styles by using simple language, avoiding jargon, and providing context. Visual cues and non-verbal communication are also crucial, as they can be difficult to interpret in text or video. Regular video meetings can provide a more personal and nuanced form of communication. Discipline and self-motivation are also essential, as remote collaboration can lead to isolation and distraction. Establishing a dedicated workspace separates work from personal life, maintaining a work-life balance and ensuring productivity doesn't suffer. In conclusion, remote collaboration offers both opportunities and unique challenges. By utilizing the right tools and techniques, effective remote communication, task management, and collaboration can be achieved. Fostering a cohesive team culture is crucial for a thriving distributed team.

Balancing Individual Productivity and Team Collaboration

Balancing individual productivity and team collaboration is a crucial skill in the programming world, where deadlines and ever-changing requirements are essential. To optimize productivity, one must analyze their current time management and identify areas for improvement. Setting realistic goals and prioritizing tasks is essential for setting clear objectives for work and ensuring both individual success and team contribution. Striking a balance between ambition and feasibility is crucial to avoid burnout and ensure efficient allocation of time and energy.

Achieving a balance also requires personal growth as a programmer. Staying updated with rapid advancements and innovations in the field expands knowledge and enhances contribution to the team. Continuous learning and exploring new technologies, frameworks, and methodologies can bring fresh perspectives and ideas to the collaborative process. Actively seeking feedback and embracing constructive criticism can help refine skills and evolve as a developer.

In an increasingly interconnected and fast-paced industry, collaboration is no longer a choice but a necessity. By investing time and effort in strengthening individual productivity and working effectively with others, one can thrive in their professional endeavors. However, achieving this balance is not without challenges. Individual productivity can be jeopardized by team collaboration demands, while excessive focus on individual work can hinder team cohesion and collective outcomes.

Effective communication is essential for maintaining alignment between individual productivity and team objectives. Regular meetings, collaboration tools, and project management software enable teams to stay connected, share progress, and address challenges. Establishing boundaries, managing interruptions, and establishing clear expectations around availability and response times can help maintain productivity while still participating in collaborative efforts.

An agile mindset, such as Scrum or Kanban, emphasizes iterative development and continuous improvement. Breaking down complex projects into manageable tasks and sprints allows team members to focus on individual productivity while contributing to the overall team effort. Frequent retrospectives and adaptability within an agile framework provide opportunities for individual growth and reflection on the collaborative process.

Indeed, mastering the delicate balance between individual productivity and team collaboration is an ongoing process that requires dedication, self-awareness, and continuous learning. It is not a one-size-fits-all approach, but rather a unique journey that every programmer must embark upon. By adopting effective time management techniques, setting realistic goals, prioritizing tasks, and nurturing personal growth, one can contribute meaningfully to their team while maintaining individual productivity.

As I reflect on my own experiences in the tech industry, I believe that finding this delicate balance is equally critical for personal fulfillment and professional success. By investing in both individual growth and effective collaboration with others, we can create a harmonious environment where innovation, productivity, and camaraderie thrive. So, embrace the challenge, prioritize the journey, and unlock your true potential as a programmer who not only excels individually but also thrives within a collaborative team.

Chapter 4: The Time Wizard

The Art of Prioritization

I have always believed that the key to success lies in one's ability to prioritize effectively. Throughout my years as a software developer, I have come to understand that being able to identify and focus on high-value tasks is crucial in achieving productivity and success. In this chapter, I will delve into the art of prioritization and how it can transform your productivity.

Understanding the Importance of Prioritization

Prioritization is crucial for programmers in the fast-paced world of technology, as it helps them stay focused on tasks that have the highest impact on their projects and goals. By prioritizing tasks, we gain direction and clarity, allowing us to differentiate between important and trivial tasks, and allocate our time and energy accordingly. This approach allows us to work smarter, not harder, by focusing on tasks that have the highest impact on our projects and goals.

Identifying High-Value Tasks

Prioritization is a crucial process in achieving project goals. It involves identifying high-value tasks that contribute the most to the project's success. This involves reviewing the project or task list and identifying tasks that align with the project's objectives. It's essential to differentiate between urgent and important tasks, as urgent tasks may require immediate attention but have minimal long-term impact. Important tasks, on the other hand, may not have an immediate deadline but are crucial for the project's success. Prioritizing high-value tasks based on their potential impact, urgency, and dependencies is crucial. It's essential to consider the consequences of not completing certain tasks on time and how they may affect the project timeline.

Managing Deadlines and Avoiding Overwhelm

Deadlines are a crucial aspect of any project, and efficient management is crucial for success. However, focusing solely on upcoming deadlines can lead to neglecting the importance of tasks. Breaking down larger tasks into smaller, manageable sub-tasks can help create a roadmap for completing tasks, meeting deadlines, and reducing stress. Time management techniques like the Pomodoro Technique can also help maintain focus and prevent burnout by directing energy towards high-value tasks.

The Pomodoro Technique

As a seasoned tech professional, I have had the privilege of working on various complex projects and managing my time effectively to consistently deliver exceptional results. One time management technique that has greatly helped me in this regard is the Pomodoro Technique. This technique, named after the Italian word for tomato, was developed by Francesco Cirillo in the late 1980s as a way to enhance productivity and manage time more efficiently.

In this step-by-step guide, I will take you through the process of implementing the Pomodoro Technique and show you how it can revolutionize your work habits. By breaking your tasks into focused intervals and incorporating regular breaks, you will experience improved efficiency, mental clarity, and ultimately, achieve your goals with ease.

Step 1: Set Your Goals and Priorities

To begin implementing the Pomodoro Technique, it is crucial to have a clear understanding of your goals and priorities. Take some time to assess the tasks at hand and determine what needs to be done. This step will help you prioritize your work and enable you to allocate the appropriate amount of time to each task. By setting achievable goals and breaking them down into manageable parts, you will be better equipped to tackle them efficiently.

Step 2: Choose a Pomodoro Interval Length

The next step in implementing the Pomodoro Technique is to determine the length of your work intervals, also known as Pomodoro intervals. Traditionally, a Pomodoro interval lasts for 25 minutes, followed by a short break of 5 minutes. However, it is important to recognize that everyone's productivity levels differ, and what works for one person may not work for another. Experiment with different interval lengths to find the optimal duration that allows you to maintain focus and productivity.

Step 3: Minimize Distractions

Distractions can significantly hinder productivity and derail your progress. To maximize the effectiveness of the Pomodoro Technique, it is essential to minimize distractions during your work intervals. Close unnecessary tabs on your browser, put your phone on silent, and create a conducive work environment. By eliminating external disruptions, you will be able to concentrate fully on the task at hand, making the most of your Pomodoro intervals.

Step 4: Start Your Timer and Focus

Once you have set your goals, chosen your interval length, and eliminated distractions, it is time to start your Pomodoro timer and dive into your work. During each Pomodoro interval, make a conscious effort to maintain focus solely on the task in front of you. Resist the temptation to switch to another task or check your emails. By dedicating your undivided attention to a single task, you will notice an increase in productivity and the quality of your work.

Step 5: Take Regular Breaks

An integral aspect of the Pomodoro Technique is the incorporation of regular breaks. After completing a Pomodoro interval, reward yourself with a short break, typically lasting 5 minutes. During this time, step away from your workstation, stretch your legs, and give your mind a rest. Allow yourself to recharge before diving into the next Pomodoro interval. These breaks not only prevent burnout but also contribute to increased mental clarity and improved focus.

Step 6: Track Your Progress

Tracking your progress is an essential part of the Pomodoro Technique. As you complete each Pomodoro interval, make a mark on a piece of paper or use a tracking app to keep a record of your accomplishments. This visual representation of your progress serves as a motivator and allows you to see how much you have achieved over time. Celebrate small victories, as they contribute to your overall productivity and drive.

Step 7: Adapt and Refine

Throughout the process of implementing the Pomodoro Technique, it is crucial to remain flexible and open to adjustments. As you continue to utilize this time management technique, you may discover that certain tasks require longer or shorter Pomodoro intervals. Be receptive to these observations and adapt your approach accordingly. The Pomodoro Technique is not meant to be rigid; rather, it serves as a framework that can be adjusted to suit your specific needs and working style.

Benefits of the Pomodoro Technique:

The Pomodoro Technique offers numerous benefits that can positively impact your efficiency and overall well-being. By incorporating this time management strategy into your work routine, you can expect the following benefits:

1. Enhanced Productivity: By breaking tasks into manageable intervals, you can work with increased focus and concentration. The Pomodoro Technique minimizes the chances of getting overwhelmed, allowing you to devote your full attention to each task and complete it more efficiently.

2. Improved Time Management: The Pomodoro Technique provides a structured approach to managing your time. By setting goals, prioritizing tasks, and allocating specific time intervals to each one, you can optimize your workflow and make the most of your available time.

3. Increased Mental Clarity: Regular breaks are essential for maintaining mental clarity and preventing burnout. The Pomodoro Technique encourages short breaks between intervals, allowing you to recharge and refocus before diving into the next task. These breaks help reduce mental fatigue, enhance creativity, and improve overall cognitive function.

4. Heightened Motivation: By tracking your progress and celebrating small victories, the Pomodoro Technique instills a sense of accomplishment and motivation. As you witness your progress over time, your confidence and motivation levels increase, contributing to a more positive work environment.

5. Improved Work-Life Balance: The Pomodoro Technique promotes a healthier work-life balance by encouraging regular breaks and preventing long stretches of intensive work. By implementing this technique, you can ensure that your work doesn't consume your entire day, leaving ample time for personal activities and relaxation.

Achieving Work-Life Balance

Work-life balance is essential for programmers to succeed in their careers and lead fulfilling lives in today's competitive society. In addition to enhancing health and wellbeing, a positive work-life balance also increases output, creativity, and job satisfaction. Programmers can revitalize their minds, stimulate creativity, and build a holistic perspective that improves problem-solving skills by making time for personal interests, hobbies, and relationships outside of the workplace.

To establish boundaries, specify precise working hours, and designate a certain area of the home for business purposes. Identifying stressors like short deadlines, difficult tasks, and high client expectations can develop effective management methods. Implementing coping strategies like mindfulness meditation, deep breathing exercises, and regular exercise can help lower anxiety and enhance general wellbeing.

Putting self-care first is essential for maintaining physical and mental well being. By taking care of ourselves, we can replenish energy levels, improve concentration, and prevent burnout, leading to increased productivity and a more sustainable work-life balance. Incorporating self-care practices into our daily lives is crucial for achieving work-life balance. This can include activities such as engaging in hobbies, spending time with loved ones, pursuing personal interests, or simply taking breaks during the workday.

Creating realistic goals and prioritizing tasks is essential for maintaining a fulfilling and sustainable lifestyle. Breaking down larger projects into smaller, manageable tasks can reduce overwhelm and maintain a sense of accomplishment. Additionally, identifying and prioritizing tasks that align with personal values and goals can help programmers maintain a healthy work-life balance.

In conclusion, achieving a harmonious work-life balance is crucial for programmers to thrive in their careers and lead a satisfying life. By implementing these strategies, programmers can create a lifestyle that nurtures both their personal and professional growth.

Chapter 5: The Resilient Mindset

Embracing Failure as a Learning Opportunity

Shift Your Perspective:

The first step in embracing failure is to shift our perspective and view it as a learning opportunity rather than a personal defeat. Failure is not a reflection of our worth as individuals or our abilities as programmers. It is merely a sign that we are pushing ourselves outside of our comfort zones and taking risks. By reframing our mindset, we can begin to see failure as a necessary part of the learning process. Every failure brings with it valuable insights and lessons that can help us grow and improve.

Extracting Valuable Lessons:

Once we have embraced failure as a learning opportunity, the next step is to extract valuable lessons from our setbacks. This requires a certain level of self-reflection and a willingness to confront our mistakes head-on. Instead of dwelling on what went wrong, we should focus on what we can learn from the experience. Did we make a technical error? Did we underestimate the complexity of the problem? By analyzing our failures, we can identify patterns and develop strategies to prevent them from happening again in the future.

Bouncing Back Stronger:

Embracing failure does not mean wallowing in self-pity or giving up on our goals. On the contrary, it is about using failure as a springboard for growth and personal development. Instead of letting failure define us, we can choose to bounce back stronger than ever before. This requires resilience, determination, and a growth mindset. Rather than seeing failure as the end of the road, we must view it as a temporary setback and an opportunity to improve our skills and knowledge. Every failure brings us one step closer to success, as long as we are willing to learn from it and keep moving forward.

Inspiring Stories:

Throughout history, countless successful programmers have faced failure and turned it into a stepping-stone towards greatness. Their stories serve as a reminder that failure is not the end of the road but a necessary part of the journey towards success. One such remarkable example is the story of Thomas Edison, the inventor of the light bulb. Edison famously said, "I have not failed. I've just found 10,000 ways that won't work." His relentless pursuit of perfection led him to discover the right way to create a working light bulb, revolutionizing the world as we know it.

Another inspiring story is that of Steve Jobs, the co-founder of Apple Inc. Jobs was famously ousted from the company he co-founded and faced numerous failures throughout his career. However, he never let these setbacks define him. Instead, he used them as an opportunity to learn and grow. It was during his time away from Apple that he launched NeXT Computer and Pixar Animation Studios, both of which eventually played a significant role in his triumphant return to Apple and the success of products like the iPhone and iPad.

These stories, along with countless others, serve as a powerful reminder that failure is not the end but a stepping-stone towards success. By embracing failure, extracting valuable lessons, and bouncing back stronger, we too can achieve greatness in our programming careers.

In the world of programming, failure is not the enemy but a necessary part of the learning process. It is through failure that we gain invaluable insights, develop resilience, and grow both personally and professionally. By shifting our perspective and viewing failure as a learning opportunity, we open ourselves up to endless possibilities and set ourselves on the path to success. So, the next time you encounter failure, remember the words of Winston Churchill, who said, "Success is not final, failure is not fatal: it is the courage to continue that counts." Embrace failure, extract its valuable lessons, and bounce back stronger than ever before. Your journey towards greatness starts now.

Managing Imposter Syndrome

Imposter Syndrome is a persistent companion that often lurks in the shadows of a programmer's mind. It is a constant reminder that despite our accomplishments, we are not worthy of success. This nagging self-doubt can have a significant impact on our programming journey, stifling our growth and holding us back from realizing our true potential. We will dive deep into the secrets of Imposter Syndrome and learn how to manage its impact on our programming journey.

The Origins of Imposter Syndrome

Imposter Syndrome is not a new phenomenon. It has plagued individuals in various fields for decades, making them question their abilities and achievements. In the realm of programming, where constant innovation and ever-evolving technologies reign supreme, it is particularly prevalent. The fast-paced nature of the industry and the pressure to keep up with the latest trends contribute to feelings of inadequacy and self-doubt.

Recognizing the Signs

The first step in managing Imposter Syndrome is recognizing its presence in our lives. It manifests itself in various ways, and we may not even realize that we are experiencing it. Common signs include:

- Constantly comparing ourselves to others and feeling inferior

- Downplaying our achievements and attributing them to luck or external factors

- Fear of being exposed as a fraud

- Setting unrealistically high standards for ourselves

- Feeling like we don't belong in our profession or team

- Overworking and over preparing to compensate for perceived inadequacies

Overcoming Self-Doubt

Once we have identified the signs of Imposter Syndrome, we can start taking steps to overcome self-doubt and build a healthier mindset. One effective technique is reframing our thoughts. Instead of dwelling on our perceived shortcomings, we can focus on our strengths and accomplishments. Celebrating our victories, no matter how small, can help us gain confidence in our abilities.

Another helpful strategy is to seek support from trusted peers or mentors. Sharing our experiences and fears with others who have been through similar struggles can provide us with a fresh perspective and reassurance. Surrounding ourselves with a supportive network of individuals who understand our journey can help us navigate the challenges of Imposter Syndrome together.

Cultivating Mental Well-being

I will share with you techniques to manage stress, anxiety, and burnout, as well as strategies to promote work-life balance, practice self-care, and build resilience. I firmly believe that by nurturing our mental well-being, we not only improve our quality of life but also enhance our creativity in the coding process.

To begin, it is essential to acknowledge the immense pressure that comes with programming. The nature of the job requires us to solve complex problems, often under tight deadlines. This constant strain can lead to stress and anxiety, which in turn can negatively impact our mental well-being. Recognizing the signs of stress and understanding how it affects us is the first step towards managing it effectively.

One of the ways I personally manage stress is by practicing mindfulness and meditation. Taking a few moments each day to sit in silence, focus on my breath, and let go of any racing thoughts has proven to be enormously beneficial. Research has shown that mindfulness and meditation can reduce stress, improve focus, and enhance overall well-being. By incorporating these practices into our daily routine, we can cultivate a sense of calm and clarity, allowing us to approach our work with a centered and relaxed mindset.

Another technique to manage stress is by practicing time management. As programmers, we often find ourselves juggling multiple projects and deadlines simultaneously. This can lead to feelings of overwhelm and burnout. By implementing effective time management strategies, such as prioritizing tasks, setting achievable goals, and creating a structured schedule, we can alleviate some of the pressure and better manage our workload. Additionally, learning to communicate boundaries and respectfully declining additional tasks when necessary is crucial for maintaining a healthy work-life balance.

Speaking of work-life balance, it is essential to make time for activities outside of programming. Engaging in hobbies, spending time with loved ones, and pursuing interests beyond the realm of technology can provide a much-needed break from the demands of the job. Research has shown that individuals who maintain a healthy work-life balance are more productive, creative, and satisfied with their work. By prioritizing time for leisure and self-care, we recharge our mental and emotional batteries, enabling us to bring fresh perspectives and new ideas to our coding projects.

Self-care is another vital aspect of cultivating mental well-being. It is important to prioritize our physical health by getting enough sleep, maintaining a nutritious diet, and engaging in regular exercise. A healthy body contributes to a healthy mind, and by taking care of our physical well-being, we are better equipped to handle the challenges that come with programming. Additionally, practicing self-compassion and allowing ourselves to make mistakes without self-judgment is crucial. Programming is a learning process, and accepting that mistakes are a natural part of growth helps foster a positive mindset and resilience in the face of setbacks.

Resilience, in fact, is an invaluable trait for programmers to develop. The ability to bounce back from failures, setbacks, and disappointments is what sets successful programmers apart. Building resilience involves cultivating a growth mindset, embracing challenges, and learning from failures. By reframing setbacks as opportunities for learning and growth, we can develop a greater sense of resilience, enabling us to persevere through difficult times and overcome obstacles with determination and grace.

Finally, it is important to recognize the profound connection between mental well-being and creativity in the coding process. When our minds are clear, focused, and at ease, we are more open to creative thinking and problem-solving. By prioritizing our mental well-being, we unlock our full potential as programmers and tap into our innate creativity. This creativity fuels innovation, enabling us to find imaginative solutions to complex problems and elevate the quality of our work.

In conclusion, prioritizing mental well-being is paramount for programmers to thrive in their professional and personal lives. By implementing techniques such as mindfulness and meditation, time management, work-life balance, self-care, and resilience-building, we can nurture our mental well-being and enhance our creativity in the coding process. Remember, taking care of ourselves is not only essential for our personal happiness and fulfillment but also crucial for our professional success. So, let us commit to cultivating mental well-being and embark on a journey of self-discovery and growth as programmers with the programmer's mindset.

The Power of Positive Mindset

To truly harness the power of a positive mindset, one must first recognize the importance of optimism. Optimism is the belief that things will work out for the best, even in the face of challenges or setbacks. In the realm of programming, it is essential to approach complex problems with a can-do attitude. Instead of seeing obstacles as insurmountable barriers, an optimist views them as opportunities for growth and improvement.

One technique that has helped me cultivate optimism is practicing gratitude. Gratitude is the act of acknowledging and appreciating the positive aspects of our lives, no matter how small they may seem. Incorporating this practice into my programming journey has allowed me to focus on the progress I have made, the skills I have acquired, and the support I have received along the way. By shifting my perspective to one of gratitude, I have been able to maintain a positive outlook even during challenging times.

Another crucial aspect of maintaining a positive mindset in programming is self-belief. Self-belief is the confidence and faith in one's own abilities and potential. Programming can be a demanding field, riddled with self-doubt and imposter syndrome. However, developing a strong sense of self-belief is vital to overcoming these obstacles and pushing through the inevitable moments of uncertainty.

To cultivate self-belief, I have found it helpful to reflect on past achievements and successes. Reminding myself of the challenges I have overcome and the solutions I have created gives me the reassurance that I am capable of conquering new coding hurdles. Additionally, seeking out positive affirmations or surrounding myself with supportive peers who believe in my abilities has made a significant impact on my self-confidence.

A positive mindset not only enhances one's problem-solving skills but also fuels creativity. When approaching programming challenges with a positive outlook, I have found that I am more open to exploring alternative solutions and thinking outside the box. By embracing the belief that there is always a solution waiting to be discovered, I have been able to come up with innovative approaches to coding problems that I may not have otherwise considered.

Moreover, a positive mindset fosters an overall sense of satisfaction in coding endeavors. When I approach my work with enthusiasm, resilience, and a belief in my abilities, the process becomes much more enjoyable and fulfilling. Programming is a continuous learning journey, and a positive mindset allows me to embrace the inevitable ups and downs without losing sight of the joy and passion I have for this field.

Research has consistently shown that a positive mindset can have a profound impact on various aspects of life, and their relevance to the programming journey is no exception. Studies have found that individuals with a positive outlook are more likely to persevere in the face of challenges and are better equipped to handle stress and setbacks. This resilience is a key attribute when it comes to programming, as projects often require long hours, debugging, and troubleshooting.

Furthermore, a positive mindset has been linked to improved cognitive abilities and increased productivity. When we approach our work with a positive attitude, our brains are more primed for learning and problem-solving. We are better able to focus, think creatively, and find solutions efficiently. This translates to more efficient coding and ultimately leads to more satisfying results.

In addition to the practical benefits, a positive mindset also has a ripple effect on our interactions with others. As programmers, we are often part of large teams, collaborating and communicating to bring projects to fruition. A positive and optimistic attitude can create an environment of trust, collaboration, and open-mindedness. It encourages healthy and constructive communication, fostering a supportive atmosphere where everyone can thrive and contribute their best work.

Cultivating a positive mindset is not a one-time task; it is an ongoing process that requires dedication and practice. However, the rewards are well worth the effort. By harnessing the power of a positive mindset, programmers can unlock their full potential, overcome challenges with resilience, ignite creativity, and ultimately find greater satisfaction in their coding endeavors.

In conclusion, a positive mindset can make a world of difference in the programming journey. By embracing optimism, practicing gratitude, and cultivating self-belief, programmers can enhance their problem-solving skills, unlock their creativity, and find greater satisfaction in their work. It is a journey that requires constant effort, but the rewards are immeasurable. So, as you embark on your coding endeavors, remember the power that lies within a positive mindset and let it guide you towards success and fulfillment.

Nurturing Your Passion for Programming

One of the key elements to ensuring a sustainable passion for programming is to constantly seek inspiration. In the ever-evolving world of technology, there is always something new to learn and explore. I have found that staying up to date with the latest trends and advancements in the programming realm not only keeps me engaged, but also sparks new ideas and possibilities in my work.

To fuel my inspiration, I regularly attend tech conferences and meet-ups where professionals from various fields come together to share their knowledge and experiences. These events not only provide valuable insights and techniques but also serve as a reminder of the vast opportunities that lie ahead in the coding world.

Additionally, I make it a point to read books and articles related to programming, particularly those written by industry experts. These resources not only expand my knowledge but also offer different perspectives and approaches to problem-solving. Exploring different programming languages and frameworks also helps me stay motivated, as it broadens my skillset and enables me to tackle a wider range of projects.

Setting meaningful goals is another crucial aspect of nurturing your passion for programming. Without clear objectives, it can be easy to lose direction and motivation along the way. When setting goals, it is important to make them specific, measurable, attainable, relevant, and time-bound, also known as SMART goals.

For example, rather than simply aiming to learn a new programming language, I would set a SMART goal such as "Become proficient in Java within six months by completing an online course, building a small project, and contributing to an open-source repository." This type of goal provides a clear roadmap and benchmarks to track progress, which ultimately leads to a sense of accomplishment and satisfaction.

In addition to setting long-term goals, I also find it helpful to break them down into smaller, more manageable milestones. This approach allows me to celebrate achievements along the way and maintain a sense of momentum. Celebrating these small wins not only boosts morale but also reinforces the belief that continuous progress is being made.

Another effective strategy to nurture your passion for programming is to find joy in the process. Coding can be complex and challenging, but it is also a creative and problem-solving endeavor. Embracing the mindset of a craftsperson, I immerse myself in the process, appreciating the small victories and learning from the setbacks.

When faced with a difficult coding problem, I remind myself that every challenge is an opportunity for growth and learning. I approach coding with a sense of curiosity and excitement, knowing that each line of code brings me closer to a solution. This mindset shift has not only made programming more enjoyable but has also enhanced my ability to persevere in the face of obstacles.

Additionally, I find it helpful to cultivate a supportive network of fellow programmers and mentors. Connecting with like-minded individuals allows me to share knowledge, seek advice, and learn from their experiences. Surrounding myself with a community of passionate coders who understand the ups and downs of the coding journey has been invaluable in sustaining my motivation and enthusiasm.

However, it's important to remember that the coding journey is not without its challenges. There will inevitably be times when frustration sets in and progress seems elusive. During these moments, it is vital to maintain a growth mindset and view setbacks as opportunities for improvement.

One technique I employ to navigate these challenges is the use of positive affirmations and visualization. I remind myself of past successes and envision myself overcoming the current obstacle. This not only helps me stay focused and motivated but also boosts my confidence and belief in my abilities.

Taking breaks and allowing yourself to recharge is also essential. Programming requires intense focus and problem-solving, which can be mentally draining. Stepping away from the computer and engaging in activities that bring you joy and relaxation allows you to return to your work with renewed energy and enthusiasm.

Finally, it's critical to strike a balance between your personal and professional lives. While having a strong enthusiasm for coding is wonderful, spending too much time and effort on it might result in burnout. You may retain a positive outlook and avoid programming from being all-consuming by giving self-care a high priority and scheduling time for hobbies, relationships, and other interests.

To sum up, it takes a combination of motivation, goal-setting, endurance, and self-care to nurture your passion for programming. You may keep your motivation up and experience joy and fulfillment in the process by implementing these strategies into your journey toward learning to code. Recall that programming is an attitude as much as a talent. Accept the difficulties, rejoice in the successes, and keep developing as a programmer.

Chapter 6: The Curious Coder

The Joy of Learning

We will go into the significance of finding the joy of learning and its crucial part in your quest to learn how to code. We'll look at a number of strategies that can help you develop an attitude of curiosity, accept new technology, and broaden your knowledge base. We'll also explore how creativity and curiosity are intrinsically linked to the coding process.

1. Getting Started with the Joy of Learning

Learning is a lifetime process, and we programmers have the benefit of working in a constantly changing industry. The excitement of learning comes from continually discovering new ideas, tools, and methods that can improve our coding skills. This happiness is what drives our enthusiasm for programming and keeps us inspired to keep getting better and better.

2. Fostering an Inquisitive Mindset:

The development of a curious attitude is crucial for unlocking the joy of learning. Our need to learn and our motivation to look for fresh data and insights are both driven by curiosity. Thankfully, curiosity is a quality that can be developed and fostered.

One strategy for encouraging curiosity is to  approach every coding task with a sense of wonder and intrigue. Instead of viewing a problem as a mundane task, see it as an opportunity to explore new possibilities and solutions. Embrace the mindset of a beginner, always eager to learn, experiment, and ask questions. Curiosity will fuel your passion and drive, making the learning process enjoyable and rewarding.

3. Adopting Modern Technology

New technologies regularly appear in the dynamic world of programming, providing exciting prospects for development and innovation. It is essential to embrace these new tools with an open mind and a readiness to experiment if you want to truly appreciate the thrill of learning.

Keeping up with market developments and trends is one efficient strategy to adopt new technologies. Follow tech blogs, sign up for newsletters for developers, and take part in online forums and communities that are focused on your interests. Your knowledge will grow as a result of this ongoing exposure to new concepts and technologies, which will also encourage you to think creatively and push the limits of your coding abilities. Attending technological conferences and seminars can also present beneficial chances to learn from authorities in the field and network with like-minded individuals. These events often showcase the latest innovations and offer hands-on experiences that can enhance your understanding and proficiency in new technologies. By actively seeking out these learning opportunities, you can stay ahead of the curve and continually adapt to the ever-evolving tech landscape.

4. Broadening Our Knowledge Base

While staying current with technology is important, it's also crucial to expand your knowledge beyond your core programming language or area of expertise. Your mind can be stimulated, and new views on problem-solving can be provided by learning new languages, frameworks, and methodologies.

Investigating several programming languages is one way to broaden your horizons in terms of knowledge. Every language has distinctive characteristics and paradigms that can help you better understand programming ideas and increase the breadth of your toolkit. Consider studying related disciplines like cyber security, machine learning, or data analysis as well. Your programming skills will improve thanks to this multidisciplinary approach, which will also give you access to exciting job options.

5. The Connection between Curiosity and Creativity:

The two qualities of curiosity and creativity go hand in hand. Creativity and problem-solving are made possible when we foster our curiosity. The excitement of learning comes from the capacity to think creatively, to question received wisdom, and to solve challenging programming issues.

It takes a willingness to explore, take chances, and think outside the box to embrace curiosity and creativity in the coding process. Allow oneself to consider alternative viewpoints and approaches rather than tackling a subject from a single, fixed point of view. Be open to adding fresh concepts to your own coding methods while taking in other people's varied experiences and viewpoints. You will improve your coding abilities and get a ton of fulfillment if you embrace inquiry and innovation. the process.

6. Sharing knowledge is fun.

As programmers, we have the exceptional chance to add to the body of collective knowledge in our community. Sharing knowledge improves not only the lives of others around us but also our own comprehension and command of programming principles.

Sharing your knowledge, experiences, and lessons gained can have a significant impact on your coding journey, whether it is through blogging, giving presentations at conferences, or taking part in online forums. You are compelled to clarify your own understanding, spot knowledge gaps, and consider fresh learning opportunities through the act of teaching and explaining topics. Additionally, by imparting your knowledge, you actively contribute to the expansion and advancement of the programming community as a whole.

7. Final thoughts:

I hope that by reading this, you will be motivated to learn and to appreciate learning's value as you embark on a coding career. You can maximize the potential of your programming abilities by developing a curious mentality, adopting new technologies, broadening your knowledge base, and embracing curiosity and creativity. Never forget that learning is a lifelong journey that enables us to continuously improve, invent, and delight in the dynamic world of programming. Accept this thrill and allow it to lead you to become a true code craftsman.

Chapter 7: The Harmonious Coder

Healthy Habits for Coders

Let's look at how good habits can improve your coding abilities. Even though coding frequently entails spending long hours in front of a screen, including exercise, wholesome foods, and sufficient sleep into your routine will boost your mental performance and general wellbeing.

Exercise Boosts Your Brain and Mood

Regular exercise isn't just for health-conscious people. It acts as a brain enhancer! Exercises that increase blood flow to the brain, such as running, swimming, or yoga, help you become more alert and creative. Additionally, exercise causes the production of "feel-good hormones" that lower stress and improve mood.

Make Exercise Part Of Your Routine

Though it may be challenging, making time for exercise is worthwhile. Set up fitness sessions and choose enjoyable hobbies. Don't forget to take little walks or stretches throughout your work breaks. It's not only about your health; it also boosts productivity and minimizes burnout.

Mindful Movement Matters

In addition to routine exercise, consider meditative activities like yoga or tai chi. They're like a double espresso for your mind; they're not simply excellent for your body. You may unwind, relieve stress, and improve your physical and mental wellbeing by engaging in these hobbies.

Nutrition for Brainpower

The functioning of your brain is greatly influenced by food. Your brain gets a boost from nutrients like omega-3 fatty acids, antioxidants, and vitamins (including B, C, and

E), making you sharper and more focused. On the other hand, junk food, sweets, and unhealthy fats can slow you down and muddle your thinking.

Build A Balanced Diet

Start by making wise eating choices. Put fresh produce, whole grains, lean proteins, and healthy fats on your dish. Plan your meals in advance to ensure that you have wholesome options on hand even during extended periods of coding. Drink plenty of water; maintaining hydration is crucial for optimal brain performance.

Eat Mindfully Matters

It's simple to eat snacks while coding in our fast-paced digital world. Try, nonetheless, to eat slowly. Enjoy your meals, eat quietly, and pay attention to your body's signals of hunger and fullness. It enables you to choose healthier foods, curb overeating, and appreciate the nourishment you're giving your body.

The Sleep Trick

For your brain, a good night's sleep is like a magic wand. Your brain absorbs information, stores memories, and gets ready for the day while you sleep. Your brain sputters when you don't get enough sleep, which makes you less productive and more prone to mistakes.

Set A Sleep Routine

Set up a regular sleep schedule by going to bed and waking up at the same time each day. Make a peaceful, cozy, and dark environment that is conducive to sleeping. Before going to bed, unwind with peaceful pursuits like meditation, a warm bath, or reading. Make sleep a priority, and you'll awaken feeling rejuvenated and prepared to take on your coding difficulties.

Healthy Lifestyle, Sharp Mind

Your ability to think clearly will be greatly enhanced if you incorporate regular exercise, a healthy diet, and adequate sleep into your daily routine. Your brain gets a boost from exercise, nutrition supports memory and concentration, and sleep allows your brain to recover.

Boost Productivity

Not only can healthy habits help you feel better, but they also increase your productivity while coding. While adequate nutrition helps to preserve mental clarity, exercise and thoughtful breaks help to increase focus and creativity. A good night's sleep revitalizes your brain, preparing you for success in coding.

Happiness in Health

A healthy lifestyle has psychological advantages as well as physical ones. Exercise causes the release of "feel-good hormones," which lower stress and increase general happiness. Emotions are stabilized by nutrient-rich diets, while mood and wellbeing are improved by getting enough sleep.

Chapter 8: The Future of Code Craft

Emerging Technologies

One of the most buzz worthy and impactful emerging technologies in recent times is artificial intelligence (AI). AI has come a long way from being a concept confined to science fiction movies to becoming a reality that has the potential to revolutionize the programming industry. AI, in its simplest form, refers to the ability of machines to mimic human intelligence and perform tasks that traditionally require human intelligence. This includes tasks such as speech recognition, image processing, pattern recognition, and even decision-making. The applications of AI in programming are vast and varied, ranging from automated code generation to intelligent debugging and even predicting software defects before they occur. As AI continues to evolve, I always make it a point to stay updated on the latest developments in this field, as it has the potential to significantly enhance my programming skills and improve the efficiency of my work.

Another emerging technology that has garnered a lot of attention in recent years is blockchain. Originally introduced as the underlying technology behind Bitcoin, blockchain has now emerged as a powerful tool that has the potential to transform industries beyond just finance. At its core, blockchain is a decentralized and tamper-proof digital ledger that records transactions across multiple computers. This technology eliminates the need for intermediaries in various domains, increasing transparency and security while reducing costs and the probability of errors. As a programmer, understanding the fundamentals of blockchain is essential, as it opens up new avenues for creating decentralized applications, smart contracts, and secure data transfer protocols. Exploring blockchain technology and its integration with programming languages such as Solidity and Ethereum provides me with the necessary skills to develop applications that leverage the power of blockchain.

Internet of Things (IoT) is yet another emerging technology that is poised to transform the way we interact with technology and our physical surroundings. IoT is essentially a network of interconnected devices that communicate and exchange information with each other over the internet. This network encompasses everyday objects such as refrigerators, thermostats, cars, and even wearable devices. The possibilities with IoT are limitless, as it enables automation, improved efficiency, and even predictive maintenance. As a programmer, understanding how to develop applications that interface with IoT devices and leverage their data is of paramount importance. This includes programming in languages such as C++ and Python, as well as understanding protocols like MQTT and CoAP. By exploring the world of IoT, I not only gain a deeper understanding of the potential applications but also uncover ways to integrate IoT with other emerging technologies, such as AI and blockchain, to create even more powerful and innovative solutions.

Beyond these three major emerging technologies, countless other advancements are reshaping the programming landscape. From virtual reality and augmented reality to quantum computing and edge computing, the possibilities are truly endless. As a programmer, it's vital to stay updated on these emerging technologies and understand their potential applications and implications. Fortunately, there are several techniques that can help me and other programmers stay abreast of the latest trends.

One of the most effective ways to stay updated is by regularly attending industry conferences and networking events. These events provide a platform for industry experts and thought leaders to share their knowledge and insights into emerging technologies. Additionally, they offer an opportunity to network with other professionals and exchange valuable information and experiences. By engaging in these events, I can gain firsthand knowledge of the latest advancements and even collaborate with like-minded individuals to explore new avenues and possibilities.

Another technique that I find invaluable in staying updated on emerging technologies is continuous learning. The tech industry is constantly evolving, and if I want to remain relevant and competitive, I need to continuously invest in my skills and expand my knowledge base. This involves regularly reading research papers, books, and online resources dedicated to emerging technologies. Additionally, I make it a point to enroll in online courses and certifications that provide in-depth knowledge and practical skills in these areas. Continuous learning not only keeps me informed but also ensures that I have the necessary tools to harness the power of emerging technologies and translate them into tangible solutions.

Participating in online communities and forums is also a great way to stay updated and engage in conversations surrounding emerging technologies. These platforms provide a space for programmers from all around the world to share their experiences, ask questions, and discuss the latest trends. By actively participating in these communities, I can gain insights from others, share my own knowledge, and even collaborate on projects that utilize emerging technologies. The power of collective intelligence cannot be underestimated, and these communities provide a platform for harnessing that power.

In conclusion, exploring the exciting world of emerging technologies is crucial for any programmer who wishes to stay ahead of the curve. Understanding and harnessing the power of artificial intelligence, blockchain, Internet of Things, and other emerging technologies can open up new avenues for innovation and enhance the efficiency and effectiveness of programming. By staying updated through various techniques such as attending conferences, continuous learning, and participating in online communities, I ensure that I am always ready to embrace the potential of emerging technologies and translate them into tangible solutions. The programming landscape is constantly evolving, and it is up to us programmers to adapt and embrace the endless possibilities that emerging technologies bring.

Ethical Considerations in Code Craft

As a programmer, it is essential to understand and explore the ethical considerations that come with code craft. In today's world, where technology impacts every aspect of our lives, it becomes imperative to prioritize privacy, data security, and responsible use of technology. In this chapter, we will delve deep into the ethical implications of code craft and learn techniques to develop software with integrity, empathy, and social impact in mind.

Privacy: Respecting User Confidentiality

Privacy is a fundamental right of individuals, and as code crafters, we must treat it with utmost respect. When developing software and web applications, we need to consider the data we collect and how we handle it. It is crucial to inform users about the information we collect and obtain their consent before doing so.

In my years of experience as a data analyst, I have come across numerous situations where companies have collected personal data without proper consent or misused it for their own benefit. This not only violates user trust but also raises serious ethical concerns. As programmers, we should prioritize user privacy and ensure that the data we collect is used responsibly and securely.

To achieve this, implementing privacy policies and utilizing encryption techniques are crucial. Privacy policies should clearly communicate the data collection practices, storage methods, and intended use of the collected information. By encrypting sensitive user data, we can protect it from unauthorized access and ensure its confidentiality. It is essential to stay updated with privacy regulations and diligently follow them to promote a culture of privacy-centric code craft.

Data Security: Safeguarding Information Assets

Data security is another crucial aspect of ethical code craft. When developing software, we often deal with sensitive information, such as personal details, financial data, or medical records. It is our responsibility to ensure that this data is protected from unauthorized access, manipulation, or theft.

To achieve robust data security, we must consider various factors. First and foremost, adhering to best practices for secure coding is vital. By following programming guidelines and applying secure coding practices, we can reduce vulnerabilities and strengthen the overall security of our software.

Implementing strong authentication and access control mechanisms is also crucial. By properly verifying and authenticating users, we can prevent unauthorized access to sensitive data. Additionally, regular security assessments, such as penetration testing, can help identify vulnerabilities and address them before they can be exploited.

Lastly, data encryption is an invaluable tool in ensuring data security. By encrypting data at rest and in transit, we can protect it from unauthorized disclosure. Encryption algorithms such as SSL/TLS for data in transit and AES for data at rest can significantly enhance the security of our software.

Responsible Use of Technology: Considering the Ethical Implications

As programmers, we have a responsibility to use technology in a manner that is ethical and responsible. Emerging technologies such as artificial intelligence, machine learning, and big data analytics have enormous potential to drive social impact. However, if not carefully handled, they can also perpetuate biases, invade privacy, or infringe on individual freedoms.

Developing software with integrity, empathy, and social impact in mind requires us to be conscious of the potential ethical implications of the algorithms we create and the data we use. It is important to continually assess the ethical consequences of our code and make conscious efforts to mitigate any negative effects.

One particular area of concern is algorithmic bias. Algorithms are often trained on large datasets that may contain inherent biases, leading to biased decisions. As code crafters, it is our responsibility to identify and address these biases, ensuring that our software treats users fairly and impartially. By diversifying the dataset used for training and employing fairness metrics, we can eliminate bias and promote social equality.

Additionally, we must also consider the impact of our software on the environment. The technology industry contributes to a significant carbon footprint, and as programmers, we can play a part in minimizing it. By optimizing code for energy efficiency, designing sustainable software architectures, and promoting responsible data storage practices, we can reduce the environmental impact of our software.

Developing Software with Social Impact

Finally, developing software with social impact requires us to consider how our code can be used to address societal challenges and improve the lives of individuals and communities. By leveraging our technical skills, we can create applications that promote education, healthcare, accessibility, and sustainability.

For example, developing educational software that enhances access to quality education for marginalized populations can have a positive social impact. Similarly, creating healthcare applications that improve access to medical information or connect remote areas with healthcare providers can significantly enhance healthcare outcomes.

When developing software with social impact in mind, it is essential to involve the intended users and stakeholders throughout the process. By actively seeking their input and incorporating their needs and perspectives, we can ensure that our software truly addresses their challenges and empowers them.

Exploring ethical considerations in code craft is a crucial part of being a responsible programmer. By prioritizing privacy, data security, and responsible technology use, we can develop software with integrity, empathy, and social impact in mind. Privacy policies, secure coding practices, and data encryption are essential techniques to protect user confidentiality and safeguard information assets. Considering the ethical implications of our algorithms and actively working to mitigate biases ensures fairness and equality. Developing software with social impact requires involving users and stakeholders and leveraging technology to address societal challenges. As programmers, it is our responsibility to continuously learn, adapt, and evolve to create a positive and ethical tech ecosystem.

Embracing Continuous Learning in the Digital Age

In today's dynamic digital landscape, change is the only constant. Technology evolves at an astonishing pace, demanding that programmers adapt and grow to remain relevant. Lifelong learning emerges as the vital tool enabling us not just to keep up with this ever-shifting landscape but to thrive within it. This journey explores the significance of lifelong learning, offering insights and strategies to equip you for a successful and ever-evolving career in programming.

The Significance of Lifelong Learning

With over 18 years of experience as a tech professional, I've witnessed firsthand the profound impact of continuous learning. The world of programming operates at breakneck speed. Relying solely on skills acquired in school or early careers becomes obsolete. Technology marches forward, tools become outdated, and new languages emerge. To remain at the forefront of this dynamic field, we must commit to lifelong learning.

Online Learning Platforms and Communities

The digital age offers unparalleled access to knowledge through online learning platforms and communities. Explore these invaluable resources to expand your skill set and stay current with the latest advancements:

1. **Coursera:** This platform features an array of courses taught by top instructors from prestigious universities and companies. From programming languages to data analysis, you'll find courses tailored to your interests and objectives.

2. **Udemy:** Udemy empowers subject matter experts to create and share courses on diverse subjects. With thousands of courses, you'll discover options catering to both novice learners and seasoned programmers.

3. **Codecademy**: Offering interactive programming courses, Codecademy promotes learning by doing. Their hands-on approach ensures practical experience as you grasp new programming concepts.

4. **Stack Overflow:** This community-driven platform serves as a hub for programmers to pose questions, seek guidance, and share knowledge. It proves invaluable for troubleshooting and learning from experienced peers.

5. **GitHub:** GitHub, renowned for version control and collaborative programming, facilitates learning through exploration. Analyzing projects on GitHub enables you to glean insights from skilled developers and contribute to open-source endeavors.

6. **ChatGPT:** Online Learning Platforms and Communities: ChatGPT, powered by OpenAI, is an AI-based language model that can provide answers to a wide range of questions, assist with learning new topics, and engage in discussions. It can be a valuable resource for acquiring knowledge and seeking guidance in various fields, including programming.

Resources for Unceasing Learning

In addition to online platforms and communities, a myriad of resources facilitate continuous learning. Consider these avenues to further your growth:

- **Podcasts:** Ideal for on-the-go learning, podcasts provide a convenient means to stay updated. Numerous programming-focused podcasts delve into industry trends, technologies, and best practices.
- **Webinars and Conferences:** Participate in webinars and conferences to stay abreast of the latest developments. These events offer opportunities to learn from industry luminaries and gain insights into emerging technologies.
- **Books and eBooks:** Books, both physical and digital, remain timeless resources for learning and self-improvement. The programming field boasts a wealth of literature covering diverse topics.
- **Online Tutorials and Documentation:** Many programming languages and frameworks feature comprehensive online tutorials and documentation. Exploring these resources deepens your understanding of specific tools and technologies.
- **Online Coding Challenges:** Engaging in online coding challenges sharpens your skills, exposes you to new problem-solving methods, and provides learning experiences based on diverse approaches.

Continuously Evolving as a Programmer

Thriving in the rapidly shifting tech landscape hinges on ongoing evolution as a programmer. Incorporate these strategies to maintain your edge:

- **Stay Curious:** Cultivate curiosity for emerging technologies and trends. Keep tabs on industry news, subscribe to relevant blogs and newsletters, and engage in meaningful conversations on social media platforms.
- **Build Side Projects:** Personal projects offer a fertile ground for exploring new technologies, experimenting with different frameworks, and applying newfound knowledge. They also showcase your adaptability and passion to potential employers.
- **Network and Collaborate:** Forge connections with fellow programmers through meet-ups, online forums, and professional networks. Collaborating with like-minded peers opens doors to fresh learning opportunities, mentorship, and career advancement.
- **Reflect and Adapt:** Routinely assess your progress, pinpoint areas for improvement, and establish self-improvement goals. Celebrate achievements, regardless of their scale, and adjust your learning strategies based on lessons learned.

The Journey Continues

Lifelong learning isn't a destination; it's a journey that extends throughout your programming career. It's a mindset that acknowledges the dynamic nature of technology and embraces the opportunities it presents. As we traverse this ever-evolving landscape, remember that each new skill acquired, each project completed, and each challenge overcome is a testament to your commitment to growth.

Embracing Continuous Growth

To sum it up, embracing lifelong learning in the digital age is not just an option; it's a necessity. The tech world will continue to evolve, presenting new challenges and opportunities. Those who embrace continuous growth will not only survive but thrive. As programmers, we have the privilege of being at the forefront of innovation. By nurturing a growth mindset, leveraging online resources, engaging with communities, and continuously evolving, we position ourselves to make a lasting impact in this dynamic field.

The Time is Now

The digital age is characterized by unprecedented access to knowledge and resources. The barriers to learning have never been lower. With dedication and commitment, you can acquire new skills, deepen your expertise, and become a driving force in the tech industry. The time to embark on your lifelong learning journey is now.

Conclusion

In 'Code Craft: The Mindset of a Programmer,' we've embarked on a journey to uncover the fundamental principles that define exceptional developers. We've explored the art of logical thinking and the mastery of problem-solving, recognizing that these skills are the bedrock of code craft. We've emphasized the importance of perpetual learning, understanding that in the ever-evolving landscape of technology, the pursuit of knowledge is unending.

We have embraced the delicate balancing act between creativity and accuracy throughout this journey, learning that clean code is not only functional but also attractive. Since good communication and version control are crucial for success, we have harnessed the power of collaboration in both teams and the lone world of coding.

To achieve a healthy work-life balance, we've mastered the art of time management, including the Pomodoro Technique and prioritization. We've studied the resilient mindset, realizing that failure is not a barrier to growth but a stepping stone in the right direction and that mental health and happiness are essential allies in the process of learning to code.

As inquisitive programmers, we have loved learning while being mindful that the quest for knowledge is an ongoing experience. Finally, after considering how code craft will develop in the future, we can welcome constant learning in the digital world because of new technology and ethical issues.

We've laid the groundwork for mastering the art of programming as well as the art of being a programmer in this series, "The Programmer's Mindset." With these principles as your compass, you are not only prepared to write code but also to create elegant, useful, and creative code. As we wrap up this chapter, keep in mind that the mindset of a programmer is more than just a set of abilities; it's a way of life. So, go forward with an open mind, a strong will, and an unwavering commitment to continuous learning, for these are the hallmarks of true code craftsmanship.

Congratulations on completing your book!

About The Author

Oladeji Afolabi has over 18 years of experience as a seasoned software and online application developer and data analyst. He is renowned for carrying out strategic plans, supervising challenging projects, and producing excellent outcomes.

Oladeji is a highly successful professional with competence in system analysis, software project management, and leadership. He is skilled in web scraping, data analysis, Python, PHP, JavaScript, and SQL. He also has a mathematical background.

Outside of his technical expertise, Oladeji is a prominent local figurehead in certain humanitarian organizations.